FLORIOGRAPHY

FLORIOGRAPHY

An Illustrated Guide to the
Victorian Language of Flowers

Jessica Roux

Andrews McMeel
PUBLISHING®

Andrews McMeel Publishing
a division of Andrews McMeel Universal
1130 Walnut Street, Kansas City, Missouri 64106

www.andrewsmcmeel.com

24 25 26 27 28 TEN 15 14 13 12 11

ISBN: 978-1-5248-5814-8

Library of Congress Control Number: 2020934359

Editor: Melissa Rhodes Zahorsky
Art Director/Designer: Spencer Williams
Production Editor: Jasmine Lim
Production Manager: Tamara Haus

ATTENTION: SCHOOLS AND BUSINESSES
Andrews McMeel books are available at quantity discounts with bulk purchase for educational, business, or sales promotional use. For information, please e-mail the Andrews McMeel Publishing Special Sales Department:
sales@amuniversal.com.

CONTENTS

For my sister, Liana, whose name is derived from a climbing vine:
you taught me how to climb and were there to catch me when I fell.

INTRODUCTION

Chrysanthemums are for condolences, rue is for regret, and rosemary is for remembrance.

The Victorian language of flowers—also called floriography—emerged as a clandestine method of communication at a time when proper etiquette discouraged open and flagrant displays of emotion. First emerging in 1819 with Charlotte de la Tour's *Le langage des fleurs*, this coded "language" was used widely throughout the nineteenth century in both England and America and today is synonymous with Victorian tradition and culture. Flower meanings were taken from literature, mythology, religion, medieval legend, and even the shapes of the blooms themselves. Often, florists would invent symbolism to accompany new additions to their inventory, and occasionally, flowers had different meanings depending on the location and time. Young women of high society in this era embraced the practice, sending bouquets as tokens of love

or warning, wearing flowers in their hair or tucked into their gowns, and celebrating all things floral. Many of them created small arrangements of flowers, called tussie-mussies or nosegays, by combining a few blooms in a small bouquet. Worn or carried as accessories, these coded messages of affection, desire, or sorrow allowed Victorians to show their true feelings in an enigmatic and alluring display.

As the era came to an end and the First World War began, the language of flowers faded in popularity. Traces of the tradition remain, however. We still use roses to convey love at weddings and on Valentine's Day, lilies for peace, and mums for condolences. The elegance and beauty of flowers have not dwindled—only our knowledge of their coded meanings. I hope this book, apart from offering a view into the history of floriography, will encourage readers to look at flowers and herbs in a new way, perhaps assigning their own meanings to the blooms that inspire them most.

FLOWERS

AMARYLLIS

Hippeastrum

Meaning:
Pride

Origin:
The Victorians associated amaryllis with pride by virtue of its grand, tall stalks topped with bright blooms that towered over other flowers. Amaryllis, with its often leafless stems, is also known for withstanding drought. It is a strong and hearty plant, too prideful to perish under harsh conditions.

Pair with . . .
Hydrangea to indicate boastful pride

Clematis to show the recipient should be proud of their cleverness

ANEMONE

Anemone

Meaning:
Forsaken love

Origin:
The anemone's association with forsaken love can be traced back to Greek mythology. The flower is said to have sprung from Aphrodite's tears as she mourned the loss of her beloved Adonis. He was killed by the jealous gods over his relationship with the goddess of love.

Pair with . . .
Camellia to show longing for what could have been

Yarrow to help heal a broken heart

APPLE BLOSSOM

Malus

Meaning:
Preference

Origin:
The apple's connection to preference comes from the fable of the Golden Apple of Discord. Eris, the goddess of discord, threw a golden apple into a wedding ceremony that she was not invited to attend. The apple was inscribed with "For the most beautiful," and Hera, Athena, and Aphrodite all laid claim to it. Zeus tasked Paris of Troy with deciding between the three goddesses. He eventually chose Aphrodite after she promised him the love of the world's most beautiful woman, Helen of Sparta. Because Helen was already married to King Menelaus, Paris's preference ultimately caused the Trojan War.

Pair with . . .
Pansy to show the recipient you're thinking of them

Zinnia for a gift for a best friend

ASPHODEL

Asphodelus

Meaning:
My regrets follow you to the grave

Origin:
In Greek mythology, asphodels grew in the underworld and were consumed by the dead. Homer's *Odyssey* shaped the idea of asphodel as a flower of regret, referring to the Asphodel Meadows as a section of the underworld where neither good nor evil souls resided—a type of ghostly purgatory.

Pair with . . .
Cypress or marigold to indicate mourning and despair

Rosemary to indicate eternal remembrance

ASTER

Symphyotrichum

Meaning:
Daintiness

Origin:
The aster's association with daintiness most likely comes from its appearance. The many long and slender petals delicately surround a bright, yellow center: a tiny masterpiece in a field of blooms.

Pair with . . .
Daisy for a gift for a young girl

Buttercup to compliment someone's charming demeanor

AZALEA

Rhododendron

Meanings:

Fragility

Temperance

Origin:

The azalea is notoriously fragile and difficult to grow. The beautiful, tender blossoms only last for a short time before tumbling to the ground. Along with this, its shallow roots do not tolerate overwatering, hence its association with temperance.

Pair with . . .

Mint or snowdrop to console a fragile state of mind

Heather to show the recipient will be taken care of in their time of need

BABY'S BREATH

Gypsophila

Meanings:

Purity

Innocence

Origin:

In the late nineteenth century, the *Gysophila* plant was dubbed "baby's breath," due to its lovely scent and small, delicate blooms. Similar in appearance to the intricate lace of a bridal veil, this flower is frequently used in wedding bouquets as well as in arrangements for new mothers.

Pair with . . .

Lily as a gift for new parents

Queen Anne's lace as a gift for a godparent, to thank them for protecting and caring for the child

BASIL

Ocimum

Meaning:
Hate

Origin:
Basil's association with hate comes from the Greeks, who believed the plant's unfolding leaves to resemble the basilisk's opening jaws. The Greeks also associated hatred with the basilisk's glare, because this legendary serpent could kill with just one glance.

Pair with . . .
Lavender for betrayal

Oleander as a warning to someone you distrust

BEGONIA

Begonia

Meanings:

To repay a favor

A warning

Origin:

To repay a favor, Charles Plumier, a seventeenth-century French botanist, named the begonia flower after Michel Bégon, a French politician and plant collector. The flower's name, which contains the phrase "be gone," may explain its use as a symbol of warning.

Pair with . . .

Sweet pea as a gift for the host of a party

Oleander to emphasize caution in a new prospect

BELLADONNA

Atropa belladonna

Meaning:
Silence

Origin:
Belladonna, also called deadly nightshade, is one of the most toxic plants on earth. It was commonly used by the Romans as a poison, causing death and thus silencing the victim forever. Additionally, the genus *Atropa* is named for the Greek goddess Atropos, the oldest of the three Fates, who was known for cutting the thread of life, ending the lives of mortals.

Pair with . . .

Columbine and begonia to urge someone to keep a secret

Rue to warn the recipient to keep quiet lest they regret it

BLUEBELL

Hyacinthoides

Meanings:

Humility

Faithfulness

Origin:

The bluebell's appearance inspired its associations with humility and faithfulness. The tranquil, bell-shaped flowers bow down on the stem, shying away from the sunshine as though showing contrition.

Pair with . . .

Peony for forgiveness for violating societal norms

Passionflower as a gift for someone preparing for a religious sacrament

BUTTERCUP

Ranunculus

Meaning:

You are radiant with charm

Origin:

Buttercup's meaning may originate with a Victorian-era childhood game. Children would hold a buttercup under their chin and check to see if a yellow reflection appeared on the skin. If the radiant glow appeared, then the bearer loved butter!

Pair with . . .

Cowslip to show a newfound affection

Datura to show that you will not be fooled by charm

CAMELLIA

Camellia

Meaning:
Longing for you

Origin:
The camellia's meaning originates with the 1848 Alexandre Dumas novel, *La dame aux camélias*, which tells the tragic love story of Armand Duval—a young bourgeois—and Marguerite Gautier, a courtesan. The two fall in love, but their relationship is undermined by Armand's father. Fearing scandal, he convinces Marguerite to leave Armand. Armand mourns his beloved, but he doesn't pursue her, believing she has left him for another man. Meanwhile, Marguerite falls ill with consumption. She dies alone, pining for Armand and what could have been.

Pair with . . .
Daffodil to show longing for an unrequited love

Zinnia as a gift for a friend who is moving away

CARNATION

Dianthus caryophyllus

Meaning:

Mother's eternal love

Heartache

Origin:

The meaning behind carnations can be traced back to the Crucifixion of Christ; carnations are said to have appeared where the Virgin Mary's tears fell, leading to their association with heartache and a mother's eternal love for her son. Additionally, the common name "carnation" may refer to Christ as the incarnation of God as man.

Pair with . . .

Mint or snowdrop to console the loss of a child

Heather for a child going off to college

CATTAIL

Typha latifolia

Meaning:
Peace and prosperity

Origin:
The cattail's association with peace and prosperity is largely unexplained, but it may derive from the plant's many domestic uses. Traditionally, the plant is used to weave baskets, to insulate clothing or bedding, as fuel for a hearth fire, and as food.

Pair with . . .
Wheat for a promotion at work

Laurel for success in a new venture

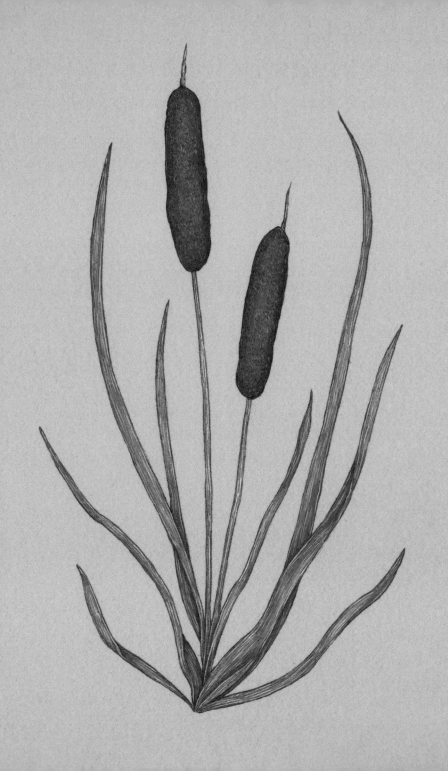

CHAMOMILE

Matricaria

Meaning:
Energy in adversity

Origin:
Chamomile's meaning may come from its many healing
properties, which were first recognized in ancient Egypt. Brewed
in tea, chamomile calms the nerves and promotes sleep, allowing
the body and mind to rest and renew during times of stress.
Chamomile is said to produce the healing energy and prolonged
vigor needed to overcome adversity.

Pair with . . .
Dogwood to show that your love will overcome all obstacles

Rose to indicate the strength of your love during a difficult time

Nettle to show sympathy for unfair circumstances

CHRYSANTHEMUM

Chrysanthemum

Meaning:
Condolences

Origin:
Autumn-blooming chrysanthemums are frequently used in funerals and placed on graves in many countries in Europe, including France, Belgium, Italy, and Spain. This ritual may derive from the practice of decorating graves on All Souls' Day, a Christian holiday occurring in early November, when many blooms are difficult to find. The chrysanthemum is thought to be a token of comfort during a time of grieving.

Pair with . . .
Willow for a friend in grief

Gladiolus for a broken heart

CLEMATIS

Clematis

Meaning:

Ingenuity

Cleverness

Origin:

Clematis, named for its cunning ability to climb up walls and trellises, is easily associated with cleverness and ingenuity. This vining bloom never fails to find its way up difficult terrain, often engulfing its surroundings once it has taken hold.

Pair with . . .

Rosemary and clover as a good luck gift before an exam

Mistletoe to show your clever problem-solving will overcome challenge

CLOVER

Trifolium

Meaning:
Good luck

Origin:
Clovers, in particular four-leaf clovers, have been associated with luck for centuries. The ancient Druids in Ireland believed that carrying a clover allowed one to detect evil spirits approaching. Similarly, in the Middle Ages, many Irish believed that carrying a four-leaf clover allowed one to see fairies. In 1620, in the earliest recorded mention of clover's association with luck, Sir John Melton wrote, "If any man walking in the fields, find any foure-leaved grasse, he shall in a small while after find some good thing."

Pair with . . .
Heather and wheat for good luck with a new business venture

Apple blossom and dandelion to show hope that the recipient's wishes will come true

COLUMBINE

Aquilegia

Meaning:
Foolishness

Origin:
Columbina was the name of a recurring character in the *commedia dell'arte* of early modern Italy. A mistress of the jester or "fool," Harlequin, Columbina was known for her loud and gossipy nature. The columbine's association with foolishness may stem from Columbina's love of the fool, or her own readiness to make a fool of herself and others. The unusually shaped bloom of the columbine also resembles a court jester's hat.

Pair with . . .
Asphodel to ask for forgiveness for an imprudent mistake

Protea to show you're working to make a big change and correct past mistakes

CORNFLOWER

Centaurea cyanus

Meaning:
Hope in love

Origin:
Folklore surrounding the cornflower, also called a "bachelor's button," states that a young man is to wear the flower when he is in love. If the flower dies quickly, it means his adoration is unrequited. However, if the flower maintains its bloom, there is hope that the young man's love will be returned.

Pair with . . .
Lilac as a gift for a first love

Sweet William to show you will always be true

COWSLIP

Primula veris

Meaning:
Winning grace

Origin:
Cowslip gets its meaning from a story told about Saint Peter, the gatekeeper of Heaven. He accidentally dropped his keys, and when they fell to Earth, they turned to cowslip. Cowslip is also known as the "key flower," because its flowers resemble a ring of golden keys. The legend suggests that those who find the flower can "win grace" and enter into Heaven.

Pair with . . .
Hawthorn for hope in a new prospect

Honeysuckle as a gift when meeting your significant other's parents

CROCUS

Crocus

Meanings:

Cheerfulness

Youthful glee

Origin:

Crocuses are some of the first flowers to bloom in the frost and snow; their cheerful petals and sunshine yellow filaments emerge to welcome spring. Perennial flowers that pop up each year, crocuses are also associated with youthful glee.

Pair with . . .

Daisy for the start of a new school year

Buttercup as a gift for a charming young friend

CYPRESS

Cupressus

Meanings:

Death

Mourning

Origin:

The cypress tree has been a symbol of mourning and death since classical antiquity, and it remains the tree most commonly planted in cemeteries in both Europe and the Middle East. In the Greek myth from which the tree gets its name, Cyparissus accidentally killed his beloved companion, a tame stag. He was so overcome by grief that he was transformed into a cypress tree.

Pair with . . .

Marigold and ivy for a grieving friend

Orange blossom to indicate your eternal devotion to a recently deceased loved one

DAFFODIL

Narcissus

Meaning:
Unrequited love

Origin:
The Greek legend of Narcissus, from which the scientific name of this plant derives, tells of a handsome and proud hunter who, upon seeing his reflection in the waters of a spring, falls in love with himself. Unable to part from his own image, he eventually perishes. A daffodil then blooms to mark his grave.

Pair with . . .
Clover for hope for change
Sweet pea to indicate giving up on an ill-suited romance

DAHLIA

Dahlia

Meanings:

Eternal love

Commitment

Origin:

The dahlia flower is often called the "Queen of the Autumn Garden" because it blooms for an extended period of time, living well into the fall months. Frequently used in wedding bouquets during the Victorian era, the flower symbolized longevity and commitment.

Pair with . . .

Tulip for a newly engaged couple

Myrtle to show love and devotion

DAISY

Bellis

Meaning:

Innocence

Childhood

Purity

Origin:

The daisy is associated with innocence, childhood, and purity in a number of folklore traditions. In Norse mythology, the daisy is tied to Freya, the goddess of fertility, motherhood, and childbirth. In Celtic tradition, daisies grew for the spirits of children who died in birth. And in ancient Roman mythology, the nymph Belides turns herself into a daisy to preserve her innocence while she's pursued by Vertumnus, the god of the seasons.

Pair with . . .

Baby's breath as a gift for a newborn baby

Peony and violet for an expression of childhood bliss

DANDELION

Taraxacum

Meaning:

Divination

Fortune-telling

Origin:

Dandelions are associated with wishes and fortune-telling; it's customary in many Western cultures to make a wish while blowing on the dandelion's "puff," dispersing its seeds. More practically, dandelions have been used to predict the weather, as their puffs will stay closed in inclement weather and open when sunny, clear skies are on the way.

Pair with . . .

Ferns for a magical solstice celebration

Foxglove and holly to indicate the ability to solve future problems

DATURA

Datura

Meaning:
Deceitful charms

Origin:
Datura, while it may charm you with its beautiful appearance, is extremely poisonous if ingested. The flowers, also known as "devil's trumpets," are said to have been used in early European witchcraft as an ingredient in the ointment that allowed witches to fly on their broomsticks.

Pair with . . .
Wormwood for a spurned lover

Thistle for a friend going through a breakup

DOGWOOD

Cornus

Meaning:
Our love will overcome adversity

Origin:
The gentle and whimsical blooms of the dogwood tree look delicate, but the wood of its trunk is strong and durable. Victorian lovers used this flower to indicate that their love could endure any trial.

Pair with . . .
Hellebore for strength to overcome scandal

Monkshood for chivalry in the face of an obstacle

EDELWEISS

Leontopodium

Meanings:

Courage

Daring

Origin:

Because the star-shaped, white edelweiss flower blooms high in the Alps, collecting the blossoms is a dangerous task. For this reason, procuring edelweiss for your lover was thought to be a feat of great courage and devotion.

Pair with . . .

Lily and laurel for a friend embarking on a new career

Sweet William to show the recipient your gallant courage

EUCALYPTUS

Eucalyptus

Meaning:
Protection

Origin:
Aboriginal peoples used eucalyptus oil to disinfect, soothe, and treat many common ailments, thus providing protection from illness. Named by Charles Louis L'Héritier de Brutelle in 1788, eucalpytus's name comes from the Greek roots *eu* and *kalyptós*, translating to "well" and "covered," again suggesting protection.

Pair with . . .
Heather for good luck to a friend embarking on a journey

Queen Anne's lace to wish the recipient safe travels

FERN

Adiantum

Meaning:

Magic

Secrecy

Origin:

Ferns grow in wet areas, yet their leaves repel water. This curious quality led ferns to be associated with magic and secrecy. The genus *Adiantum*, which comes from the Greek for "unwetted," honors ferns' fascinating duality. Additionally, Venus, the Roman goddess of love and beauty, was said to have tresses of maidenhair ferns, which remained dry after she rose from the sea.

Pair with . . .

Foxglove for a secret love

Poppy to show the recipient you think of them in your dreams

FORGET-ME-NOT

Myosotis

Meaning:

Forget me not

Origin:

The forget-me-not's name and meaning originate with a German folktale about a young couple in love. While walking along a river, the bride-to-be stops to admire a cluster of beautiful blue flowers. Her lover attempts to pick the flowers for her, but he falls into the swiftly flowing river. He throws the flowers to her as the river carries him away, calling out to her, "Forget me not!"

Pair with . . .

Zinnia for a friend who is moving away

Larkspur to say "remember the good times"

Oak for a long-distance relationship

FOXGLOVE

Digitalis

Meaning:

Riddles

Secrets

Origin:

Foxglove has long been associated with fairy folklore in the
British Isles. Its name may have been "folkglove" originally,
as fae folk—or fairies—were said to hide within its blooms.
Children who wished to see the fairies and hear their riddles
would peer inside these flowers. Picking a foxglove, however,
was thought to be bad luck, as it robbed the fairies of their
homes; this rumor may have begun to keep children from
touching these blooms, which could be deadly if consumed.

Pair with . . .

Lavender to warn a friend of an unfaithful love

Hyacinth to ask for forgiveness for divulging a secret

GLADIOLUS

Gladiolus

Meaning:

You pierce my heart

Origin:

In Latin, *gladius* translates to "sword," hence the common nickname "sword lily" for this flower. Both the name and meaning of this large and imposing plant derive from the swordlike shape of its leaves.

Pair with . . .

Yarrow to heal a broken heart

Anemone and daffodil for an unrequited love

Hemlock and marigold for a friend in grief

HAWTHORN

Crataegus

Meaning:
Hope

Origin:
In Greek mythology, Hymenaios, god of the wedding ceremony, carried a hawthorn—thought to be sacred—in a flaming torch. Ancient Greek brides used the blossoms in their bouquets and hair on their wedding days, leading to hawthorn's association with hope in love.

Pair with . . .
Camellia to indicate hope that a lost love will return

Orange blossom to show hope that the recipient will return your affections

HEATHER

Calluna

Meanings:

Luck

Protection

Origin:

Heather's meaning originates with Scottish folklore. In the
third century, Malvina, a legendary beauty, was betrothed to
a brave warrior called Oscar. As Oscar lay dying in battle, he
instructed a messenger to deliver a sprig of purple heather to
his bride-to-be as a token of his eternal love. When Malvina's
tears fell upon the flower, it changed from purple to white.
From then on, heather was said to turn sorrow to good fortune
and protection. Historically, many Scottish warriors have worn
white heather in battle for this reason.

Pair with . . .

Rose as you begin a new relationship

Cattail for good health for a friend awaiting a diagnosis

HELLEBORE

Helleborus

Meaning:
We shall overcome scandal and slander

Origin:
Despite its reputation as a poisonous plant, hellebore has been used for medicinal purposes. In Greek myth, the healer Melampus is said to have cured madness by administering hellebore, and herbalists throughout ancient times and into the Middle Ages used hellebore to treat various ailments. The curious plant, which bloomed at the very end of winter, just before spring, was thought to have magical powers, and was at times associated with witchcraft.

Pair with . . .
Begonia to warn of future challenges

Edelweiss for courage in the face of what's to come

Clover for hope and good luck

HEMLOCK

Conium maculatum

Meaning:
Death

Origin:
Hemlock is a poisonous plant that causes paralysis and death. Perhaps the most infamous poisoning by hemlock was that of Socrates, who drank a tea made from the plant after being sentenced to death for his moral philosophy.

Pair with . . .
Chrysanthemum for condolences upon the loss of a loved one

Nettle for a loved one who has been taken away too soon

HOLLY

Ilex

Meaning:
Foresight

Origin:
In many European pagan traditions, holly branches were hung in homes to protect against misfortune. This custom was later adopted for the Christmas holidays by the Victorians, who loved to indulge in superstition. Holly often figured in fortune-telling games as well; in Wales, it was said that if a girl ran seven laps around a holly tree one way, then seven times around the other way, her future husband would appear to her.

Pair with . . .
Eucalyptus to indicate looking out for a friend

Lily of the valley to show that better times are on the horizon

HONEYSUCKLE

Lonicera

Meanings:

Devotion

Affection

Origin:

Victorians claimed that sleeping with honeysuckle flowers
under your pillow would cause you to dream of your true love.
This belief may have originated with Shakespeare's *A Midsummer
Night's Dream*, in which Titania compares her slumbering with
Bottom to the way a sweet honeysuckle encircles a barky elm:
"Sleep thou, and I will wind thee in my arms . . . So doth the
woodbine the sweet honeysuckle / Gently entwist; the female
ivy so / Enrings the barky fingers of the elm. / O, how I love
thee! How I dote on thee!"

Pair with . . .

Orchid to show gratitude for a gift you treasure

Cornflower to show your true devotion to a loved one

HYACINTH

Hyacinthus

Meaning:
Please forgive me

Origin:
The hyacinth takes its name and meaning from Greek mythology. Hyacinthus, a beautiful young man, was beloved by Apollo. During a game of discus throwing, Apollo's discus was knocked from its course by a jealous Zephyrus, striking Hyacinthus and killing him. Hyacinth flowers were said to have grown from the blood that fell from his head wound as Apollo begged his forgiveness.

Pair with . . .
Olive to ask for peace and forgiveness

Pansy to indicate your betrayal haunts you

HYDRANGEA

Hydrangea

Meaning:

Boastfulness

Heartlessness

Origin:

The hydrangea's negative association with boastfulness and heartlessness comes from its bountiful and round blooms. Large and abundant, the magnificent flowers only produce a few seeds, supporting the notion that they are all show and little substance.

Pair with . . .

Tansy and petunia to indicate your displeasure at a recent turn of events

Fern to reassure a friend that you will keep their secret indiscretion to yourself

HYSSOP

Hyssopus

Meaning:
Cleanliness

Origin:
The meaning behind hyssop can be traced to ancient Greece, where the flower was used to clean and purify temples. In biblical times, the plant was even used to treat leprosy. Its cleansing aroma is a welcome addition in bouquets representing a new beginning.

Pair with . . .
Lily and Queen Anne's lace when housesitting to show you'll keep things clean and tidy

Jasmine to honor a friend for their cheerful and virtuous heart

IRIS

Iris

Meanings:

Valor

Wisdom

Faith

Origin:

The iris has long been associated with power and victory; the ancient Egyptians used the iris to crown the brow of the Sphinx. Years later, Clovis I, the fifth-century king of the Franks, won a significant battle after seeing irises blooming in a river. His soldiers adorned themselves with the flowers afterward, and the iris's three upper petals were then said to represent the valor, wisdom, and faith that led to their success in battle.

Pair with . . .

Bluebells to show humility in victory

Clematis to indicate admiration for ingenuity

IVY

Hedera

Meanings:

Fidelity

Attachment

Origin:

This clinging, leafy vine winds itself around ancient trees. Even after a tree dies, ivy remains attached, unable to be separated from its eternal embrace.

Pair with . . .

Dahlia to honor a long-lasting relationship

Hellebore to say that nothing will ever come between you and your partner

JASMINE

Jasminum

Meanings:

Amiability

Cheerfulness

Origin:

Jasmine's light and lovely scent, along with its elegantly shaped blooms, perfectly convey amiability and cheerfulness. It is often used in weddings and celebrations, especially in the Philippines, Pakistan, and Indonesia, where it is a native plant.

Pair with . . .

Iris to show admiration for a friend's strength of character

Crocus for a kind and generous loved one, or one with a particular zest for life

LADY SLIPPER

Cypripedium

Meanings:
Capriciousness

Origin:
These orchids are famously fickle and difficult to cultivate.
Some can take over a decade to bloom, and few survive
transplantation. Others, however—if left undisturbed—can live
for up to fifty years.

Pair with . . .
Hawthorn for hope for a good outcome

Snapdragon to encourage a friend in an unpredictable situation

LARKSPUR

Delphinium

Meaning:
Levity

Origin:
The distinctive seedpod of the larkspur is said to resemble the foot of a lark, hence its name. The lovely and light song of these birds lifts the spirit, just as the beautiful purple petals of the plant reach up toward the heavens.

Pair with . . .
Protea to indicate better days are ahead

Begonia to assure someone that all past problems have been reconciled

LAUREL

Laurus

Meanings:

Glory

Victory

Success

Origin:

Ancient Olympic victors were crowned in wreaths of laurel—a
tradition that was said to have originated with the Greek god
Apollo. Pursued by Apollo, the nymph Daphne begged her
father to protect her from his advances. Her father, Peneus,
answered Daphne's plea by turning her into a laurel tree. After
seeing Apollo's sadness at her transformation, Daphne is said to
have crowned him with her leaves.

Pair with . . .

Oak and edelweiss to encourage bravery in new territory

Chamomile for energy to overcome hardship

LAVENDER

Lavandula

Meaning:
Distrust

Origin:
Historically, lavender grew in hot climates, where asps—venomous snakes—frequently made their homes. Thus, the beautiful and fragrant flower could lure a curious person to their death. Some say the asp that killed Cleopatra was hidden in a bundle of lavender.

Pair with . . .
Foxglove to encourage a friend to reconsider their choices

Datura to tell someone that you see through their facade

LILAC

Syringa

Meaning:

First love

Reminiscence

Origin:

In Greek mythology, Pan, the god of the forests, was in love with Syringa, a nymph who feared his advances. To disguise herself, Syringa turned into a lilac bush. Pan, upon finding the shrub, cut its hollow reeds to form the pan flute, memorializing his first love. Victorian widows often wore lilac while in mourning over their late husbands.

Pair with . . .

Monkshood to honor your first true love

Tulip to declare being in love for the first time

Daisy and aster for the purity and innocence of one's first love

LILY

Lilium

Meaning:
Purity

Origin:
In the Middle Ages, the lily became associated with the Virgin Mary. Paintings of the Annunciation—the announcement by the archangel Gabriel to Mary that she would conceive and be the mother of Jesus—often depict Gabriel giving the Blessed Virgin a lily, in honor of her purity.

Pair with . . .
Orange blossom for a wedding anniversary

Sweet William to honor an act of pure generosity

LILY OF THE VALLEY

Convallaria

Meaning:
Return of happiness

Origin:
Saint Leonard, a hermit who lived in the forests of West Sussex, was said to have slain the last dragon in England. According to legend, the places where Saint Leonard battled the dragon are marked by lilies of the valley, which blossomed in clusters wherever the saint's blood was spilled. Once he defeated the dragon, Saint Leonard was able to resume his life of happy seclusion.

Pair with . . .
Protea to transform a bad situation into a good one

Yarrow to help soothe a broken heart

MAGNOLIA

Magnolia

Meaning:
Dignity

Origin:
The magnolia tree exudes dignity with its tall and hearty structure, its rich, waxy leaves, and its large, white blooms. Its flowers are often associated with the American South, where the tree grows to magnificent heights and endures scorching summers.

Pair with . . .
Belladonna to ask a friend to keep your secret

Olive as a reminder to maintain your dignity in difficult situations

MARIGOLD

Tagetes

Meaning:
Grief

Origin:
When clouds roll in or night falls, the marigold curls inward and lets its head droop. When it opens again in the sunlight, its petals, wet with dew, appear to be crying. Traditionally, marigolds are used to celebrate *Día de los Muertos* (Day of the Dead) in Mexico, when the spirits of the departed are believed to visit the living. This celebration is rooted in the Aztec festival honoring Mictecacihuatl, the goddess of the underworld.

Pair with . . .
Willow to indicate sorrow at the loss of a loved one

Rue to apologize for the pain you've caused

MINT

Mentha

Meaning:
Consolation

Origin:
In Greek mythology, the naiad Minthe became enamored of
Hades, the god of the underworld. Persephone, Hades's jealous
queen, turned Minthe into the common garden herb. Mint has
been associated with consolation and mourning and was often
used in funerary rites to mask the smell of the decomposing
body. And so, while Minthe could not be with the god of the
underworld, her consolation was to become a plant associated
with death.

Pair with . . .
Passionflower for faith that circumstances will improve

Cornflower to tell a friend they are thought of and loved during
a difficult time

MISTLETOE

Viscum

Meaning:
Surmounting all difficulties

Origin:
In Norse mythology, the beloved god Balder was haunted by dreams of his impending death, so his devoted mother, Frigga, made everything in nature promise not to hurt him. Sadly, she overlooked the mistletoe plant. Loki, god of mischief, created an arrow from the plant and tricked Balder's brother into killing him with it. In her grief, Frigga begged the other gods to bring Balder back, which they did, proving he could surmount all difficulties, even death itself. The now common use of mistletoe as decoration during Christmastime is a holdover from Druidic winter solstice celebrations. The bright winter berry, cut from the oak tree, was seen as a symbol of hope during the darkest, most difficult time of year.

Pair with . . .
Amaryllis for the confidence to overcome a challenge

Lady slipper to indicate your faith that the tides will turn in the recipient's favor

MONKSHOOD

Aconitum

Meaning:
Chivalry

Origin:
Monkshood is linked to chivalry thanks to the shape of its purple petals: they resemble a medieval knight's helmet.

Pair with . . .
Honeysuckle to show a friend you'll do anything for them

Dogwood or mistletoe to encourage a loved one during a tough time

Cowslip to indicate you admire someone's courage

MYRTLE

Myrtus

Meaning:

Love

Origin:

Perhaps due to their association with both Hathor and Aphrodite—Egyptian and Greek goddesses of love—the beautiful, sweet-smelling blooms of this evergreen are frequently used in wedding celebrations.

Pair with . . .

Dahlia for your one true love

Carnation for a Mother's Day gift

NETTLE

Urtica

Meaning:
Cruelty

Origin:
The stinging hairs of the nettle plant can cause painful rashes to develop on the skin. In Hans Christian Andersen's fairy tale, "The Wild Swans," a young princess named Elise must save her eleven brothers after they are turned into swans by their spiteful stepmother. In order to break the curse, Elise is instructed by a fairy to gather stinging nettles and weave them into shirts for each of her brothers. As she works in silence, the nettles cruelly sting and burn her hands. Accused of sorcery for her strange behavior, Elise is sentenced to burn at the stake. Just before she is put to death, she throws the nettle shirts over her brothers, transforming them back into men. One shirt, however, is left unfinished, leaving her youngest brother with a wing instead of an arm.

Pair with . . .
Oleander to warn someone that their betrayal has been discovered

Petunia to tell someone their apology has been deemed insincere

124

OAK

Quercus

Meaning:
Bravery

Origin:
The oak tree was perhaps the most venerated of all plants throughout much of early history. It has long been associated with brave and triumphant figures in many different cultures. In Greek mythology, the oak is the sacred tree of Zeus. In Norse mythology, it is the tree of life, revered by Thor. And in Celtic Druidic culture, the oak tree was important in many rituals and ceremonies, as it was the sacred tree of the pagan god Dagda.

Pair with . . .
Sweet William and monkshood for someone you admire

Clematis to indicate appreciation for a leader in your life

OLEANDER

Nerium oleander

Meaning:
Caution

Origin:
The Victorians assigned the meaning of "caution" to the oleander, perhaps because the plant is poisonous, but also because of its association with the Greek cautionary myth of Hero and Leander. The two were in love, and although they lived on opposite sides of the Hellespont Sea, Leander swam across it every night to visit Hero. One night, during a violent storm, Leander died while trying to swim to his love in the rough waters. When Hero saw Leander's body washed ashore, she called out, "O, Leander! O, Leander!" and drowned herself to be with him in death.

Pair with . . .
Azalea to warn someone they're about to make a poor choice

Sunflower to caution a friend against a bad investment

OLIVE

Olea

Meaning:
Peace

Origin:
To "extend an olive branch" is to offer reconciliation and peace.
This phrase comes from the Old Testament story of Noah's Ark,
in which Noah assembles an ark and fills it with pairs of animals
before a great flood. After many days at sea, he sends a dove to
search for land, and the dove returns with an olive branch in its
beak, indicating land—and peace—are near.

Pair with . . .
Hawthorn and rue to ask for forgiveness

Queen Anne's lace as a housewarming gift

ORANGE BLOSSOM

Citrus sinensis

Meaning:
Eternal love

Origin:
The orange blossom was one of the most popular wedding
flowers during the Victorian era; from simple ceremonies to
extravagant galas, almost every wedding included the orange
blossom. When Queen Victoria married Prince Albert in
1840, she wore a headdress of orange blossoms. This flower's
association with eternal love can be traced to ancient Greece:
when Hera married Zeus, she was given orange blossoms by
Gaea, the ancient goddess of the earth and fertility.

Pair with . . .
Dogwood for an anniversary gift after a difficult year

Ivy for a long-lasting relationship

ORCHID

Orchis

Meaning:

Elegance

Beauty

Origin:

The orchid's colorful, delicate, and shapely petals easily evoke elegance and beauty. The flower became an exotic luxury during the Victorian era, when only the wealthy could afford the expensive bloom.

Pair with . . .

Camellia for a friend you miss

Magnolia as a gift for someone you admire

PANSY

Viola tricolor var. hortensis

Meaning:
You occupy my thoughts

Origin:
The name "pansy" comes from the French *pensée*, meaning "thought." In Shakespeare's *Hamlet*, Ophelia remarks, "There's pansies, that's for thoughts," while distributing flowers after the death of her father.

Pair with . . .
Chrysanthemum for a loved one going through a rough time

Forget-me-not as a gift for a friend whose kindness and generosity you'll never forget

PASSIONFLOWER

Passiflora

Meaning:
Faith

Origin:
In the sixteenth century, Jesuit missionaries came across the passionflower in South America. They believed the flower to be a symbol of the Passion of Christ. The ten petals represent the ten faithful apostles, the filaments the crown of thorns, the stamens the five wounds, the ovum the hammer, and the styles the three nails that pierced the hands and feet of Christ.

Pair with . . .
Edelweiss to indicate faith that someone will make the right choice, even if it is difficult

Iris as a gift for a religious leader

PEONY

Paeonia

Meaning:
Bashfulness

Origin:
In ancient Greece, it was said that nymphs could turn themselves
into peony flowers to avoid being seen by humans. Bashful
creatures by nature, they wished to hide from mortal eyes.
Likewise, even in full bloom, peonies' petals curl inward,
protecting their delicate centers.

Pair with . . .
Hyacinth and violet to apologize and ask for forgiveness

Foxglove as a gift for a secret admirer

PETUNIA

Petunia

Meanings:

Anger

Resentment

Origin:

Little is recorded about the origin of this meaning. The petunia is sensitive and easily damaged—perhaps like a person who is filled with anger or resentment.

Pair with . . .

Wormwood to indicate displeasure at an outcome

Rosemary to show you will not forget someone's wrongdoing

POPPY

Papaver somniferum

Meaning:
Eternal sleep

Origin:
The poppy is known for its narcotic effects; it is used to make the sedative opium. According to Greek myth, poppies grew in the land of the dead. They were associated with Demeter, whose daughter, Persephone, was the queen of the underworld.

Pair with . . .
Snowdrop for the loss of a loved one

Dahlia to mark the grave of a cherished companion

PROTEA

Protea

Meaning:
Transformation

Origin:
The protea flower was named for Proteus, the son of the Greek god Poseidon. Like Proteus, who could change shape whenever he wanted, *Protea* is an extraordinarily diverse plant genus, able to take many different forms.

Pair with . . .
Laurel to congratulate a friend on their life-altering achievement

Lily of the valley as a gift for someone recovering from an illness

QUEEN ANNE'S LACE

Daucus

Meaning:
Sanctuary

Origin:
The lacy fronds of Queen Anne's lace fold together in a shield or nest-like shape, providing sanctuary and protection for their inhabitants. It is often called "bird's nest" for this reason.

Pair with . . .
Cattail for a housewarming gift

Apple blossom for a friend purchasing a new home

ROSE

Rosa

Meaning:

Love

Origin:

The rose flower has been closely linked to love in many cultures throughout history. Its lushly layered petals and sweet aroma may explain why. For the Victorians, the color of the rose indicated the level of affection: a white rose was for innocent love; a blush pink rose was for a blossoming romance; and a deep red rose for passion. In Greek myth, Chloris, the goddess of flowers, is said to have turned a beautiful, dead nymph into a rose. She invited Apollo to warm the bloom, Aphrodite to lend it her beauty, Dionysus to add sweet nectar, and the three Graces to supply charm, joy, and magnificence. Chloris called the rose the "Queen of Flowers."

Pair with . . .

Baby's breath for a wedding celebration

Cornflower for hope in a new romantic pursuit

ROSEMARY

Salvia rosmarinus

Meanings:

Remembrance

Wisdom

Origin:

Rosemary has been associated with memory since ancient Greece; to help them recall their studies, Greek scholars wore crowns of rosemary during their examinations. This symbolism was cemented with the help of Shakespeare. In *Hamlet*, during her famous "flower speech," Ophelia mentions the fragrant herb: "There's rosemary, that's for remembrance. Pray you, love, remember."

Pair with . . .

Crocus to reminisce about the past

Clematis for confidence in scholarly pursuits

RUE

Ruta

Meaning:
Regret

Origin:
While the English word "rue," meaning regret, and this plant's common name are etymologically unrelated, the Victorians still used the bitter-smelling *Ruta graveolens* to indicate regret. Most often, rue was sent, not to express regret on the part of the sender, but as a warning or threat, as in, "You'll regret what you've done."

Pair with . . .
Hyacinth to ask for forgiveness

Willow and chrysanthemum as a gift for a friend experiencing loss

SNAPDRAGON

Antirrhinum

Meaning:
Presumption

Origin:
Snapdragon's link to presumption may derive from a medieval fashion practice: maidens would wear snapdragons in their hair to show they were not interested in unsolicited attention from men. The flower warned young men against presumption in a subtle and elegant way.

Pair with . . .
Asphodel to apologize for a lack of discretion

Holly to indicate your oversight will not happen again

SNOWDROP

Galanthus

Meaning:

Consolation

Hope

Origin:

One of the first flowers to bloom in the depths of winter, the bright white snowdrop is a sign that spring—and a turn toward better, easier days—is coming. Victorians loved this unique flower but warned against bringing it into the home. If brought indoors, it was considered a bad omen, perhaps even a harbinger of death.

Pair with . . .

Carnation for a broken heart

Mistletoe to indicate endurance through difficult times

SUNFLOWER

Helianthus

Meaning:
False riches

Origin:
The ancient Inca believed this large, yellow flower to symbolize the sun god, Inti, and they decorated their bodies and temples in sunflower-shaped jewelry made of gold. As Spanish conquistadores arrived, they were impressed by this abundance of treasure, and when they saw a field of sunflowers, they believed, at first, they'd come upon a literal trove of gold. Their mistake led to the bloom's association with "false riches."

Pair with . . .
Bluebell and columbine to show humility for foolish past behavior

Lavender to indicate distrust in a business partner

SWEET PEA

Lathyrus odoratus

Meaning:
Thank you for a lovely time

Origin:
Victorians gave sweet peas to thank their hosts for an enjoyable time. The flower's light and sweet smell was believed to brighten the home and serve as a symbol of hospitality.

Pair with . . .
Hyssop and orchid to thank a friend for inviting you to their home

Zinnia as a token of appreciation

SWEET WILLIAM

Dianthus barbatus

Meaning:
Gallantry

Origin:
The origin of this flower's common name is uncertain; many have speculated that the bloom was named for various historical Williams—including William Shakespeare and William the Conqueror, among others—but no namesake has been confirmed. "Sweet William" was a common moniker for the gallant young men who featured in English folkloric stories and ballads.

Pair with . . .
Eucalyptus to show you will protect a loved one in the face of adversity

Honeysuckle to indicate commitment to a relationship

TANSY

Tanacetum vulgare

Meaning:
Hostility

Origin:
The tansy's folk medicinal uses may have given rise to its
meaning. In the Middle Ages, the plant was used in high doses
to induce abortion and treat intestinal worms. Because the
plant made people ill, in Victorian times, sending a bouquet of
tansy flowers was a way of declaring that the recipient had made
the sender sick to their stomach.

Pair with . . .
Anemone for a spurned lover

Snapdragon for someone giving you a difficult time

THISTLE

Cirsium

Meaning:
Misanthropy

Origin:
It's no surprise that the spindly, prickly thistle is associated with misanthropy. Its meaning also has biblical roots: in Genesis, when God cast Adam and Eve out of Eden, God told them that thorns and thistles would grow from the land as part of their punishment.

Pair with . . .
Rosemary to indicate you see through someone's facade

Pansy to show you're thinking of a friend going through a bitter separation

TULIP

Tulipa

Meaning:
I declare my love for you

Origin:
A Turkish legend tells of two lovers, Ferhad and Shirin, who
long to be together, but whose love is forbidden. When Ferhad
hears a rumor that Shirin has taken her own life, he kills
himself in order to be with her for eternity. Tulips—symbols of
his devotion—spring up where his blood is spilled.

Pair with . . .
Buttercup to indicate affection for a charming new love

Ivy as a gift for a newly engaged couple

VIOLET

Viola odorata

Meaning:
Modesty

Origin:
The violet grows low to the ground with its head bowed: a picture of modesty. Originally the flower of Valentine's Day, it is said that Saint Valentine, while jailed for attempting to spread Christianity, crushed violets growing near his cell in order to make ink. One legend claims he used this ink to write a letter to his jailer's daughter, whom he had healed from blindness, signing it, "Your Valentine," thus inspiring centuries of romantic notes.

Pair with . . .
Bluebell for a humble friend who means the world to you

Laurel to show a friend you're proud of their accomplishments

172

WHEAT

Triticum

Meaning:

Riches

Abundance

Origin:

Thick stalks of golden wheat have long been associated with riches and abundance. In ancient times, large stores of wheat signified wealth, and a bountiful wheat harvest was synonymous with prosperity in the coming year.

Pair with . . .

Clover for good luck in a new venture

Begonia to repay a favor

WILLOW

Salix

Meaning:
Mourning

Origin:
The weeping willow appears to be a tree in mourning; its branches are downturned and sorrowful. In Greek mythology, willows are said to mark the entrance to the underworld. This may further explain why these melancholic trees are often pictured on gravestones and Victorian mourning jewelry.

Pair with . . .
Forget-me-not and cypress for a funeral

Gladiolus for a broken heart

WORMWOOD

Artemisia absinthium

Meaning:
Bitterness

Origin:
Wormwood has a long history of association with bitterness. The Greeks called the herb *absinthium*, which translates to "bitter." Throughout the Bible, wormwood is mentioned several times, always in connection to bitterness. In the book of Revelation, it is written that a great star called Wormwood will fall from the sky and turn a third of all water bitter, causing widespread death.

Pair with . . .
Larkspur and hyacinth to tell someone that things aren't as bad as they think

Belladonna to tell a friend you'll give them space

YARROW

Achillea

Meaning:
Cure for a broken heart

Origin:
Yarrow takes its botanical name and meaning from the Greek
hero Achilles, who is said to have used a poultice of yarrow to
heal the wounds of his men on the battlefield. Yarrow is an
ancient healing plant with many medicinal properties; it is
used even today to stop bleeding, treat fevers, and promote
digestion.

Pair with . . .
Hawthorn for hope that things will get better

Protea to indicate the tide will turn in the recipient's favor

ZINNIA

Zinnia

Meaning:
Everlasting friendship

Origin:
Because zinnias are easy to grow and reseed with abundance, the Victorians associated them with everlasting friendship. A bouquet of zinnias was a common gift for a friend leaving on a trip. It was meant to convey that the friend would be missed and thought of frequently while they were away.

Pair with . . .
Jasmine to tell a friend they bring you joy

Chamomile to show appreciation for a friendship that has survived adversity

BOUQUETS

A BOUQUET FOR FRIENDSHIP

Assemble this bouquet for a best friend, as a celebration of your friendship, to brighten their day, or to let them know they're on your mind.

Combine the following in a bouquet fastened with a teal chiffon ribbon:

Zinnia for everlasting friendship

Apple blossom for preference

Pansy for a friend you think of often

Eucalyptus for protection and to strengthen the bond of friendship, so that it may last throughout the years

A BOUQUET FOR COURTING

This is the perfect bouquet to share with a new love, to thrill them or to solidify your exclusivity.

Combine the following in a bouquet fastened with a silky red ribbon:

Blush roses for a blossoming romance

Cornflower for hope in love

Sweet William for gallantry

Honeysuckle for devoted affection

A BOUQUET FOR MARRIAGE

This arrangement may be used by a bride walking down the aisle, as a gift for newlyweds, or as décor at an engagement celebration.

Combine the following in a bouquet fastened with a white lace bow:

Red roses for true love

Ivy for fidelity

Myrtle for hope and love in marriage

Dahlia for commitment and eternal love

A BOUQUET FOR SYMPATHY

Assemble this arrangement for a loved one in grief, to commemorate a loss, or as a gift of tender affection during a difficult time.

Combine the following in a bouquet fastened with a black velvet ribbon:

Chrysanthemum for condolences

Marigold for grief

Lily of the valley to show that better days are ahead

Cypress for mourning

Mint for consolation

A BOUQUET FOR REGRET AND SORROW

This bouquet is suitable for a loved one enduring heartache or separation, to comfort and console, or to remind someone that they are loved.

Combine the following in a bouquet fastened with a thin black bow:

Asphodel to indicate your regret will follow you to the grave

Azalea for fragility in a difficult time

Snowdrop for consolation and hope of better days ahead

Rue for regret

Willow for mourning

A BOUQUET FOR APOLOGY

Use this arrangement to apologize for a wrongdoing or mistake, to ask for forgiveness, or to make amends.

Combine the following in a bouquet fastened with a blue cloth braid:

Hyacinth to ask for forgiveness

Bluebell for humility

Peony for bashfulness

Olive branch to ask for peace

A BOUQUET
FOR FORGOTTEN
OBLIGATIONS

Assemble this arrangement to apologize for missing an
important celebration or for forgetting a social engagement.

Combine the following in a bouquet fastened with green garland:

Columbine for foolishness

Rue for regret

Anemone for forsaken love

Forget-me-not to indicate you won't forget again

Rosemary for remembrance

A BOUQUET FOR WARNINGS

This bouquet is useful for warning someone you distrust or indicating that trouble is on the horizon.

Combine the following in a bouquet fastened with a bright red band:

Begonia for warning

Oleander for caution

Lavender for distrust

Foxglove for secrecy

A BOUQUET FOR BITTER ENDS

This arrangement is a final, lasting reminder of your departure from a friendship or relationship that ended poorly.

Combine the following in a bouquet fastened with twine:

Petunias for anger and resentment

Datura for deceitful charms

Tansy for hostility

Thistle for misanthropy

Wormwood for bitterness

A BOUQUET FOR
NEW BEGINNINGS

This is the perfect bouquet to celebrate a new addition to the family or a new venture in someone's life. It also makes a beautiful housewarming gift.

Combine the following in a bouquet fastened with a yellow tassel:

Crocus for youthful glee

Daisy for innocence and childhood purity

Lilac for first love

Baby's breath for purity and innocence

Wheat for riches

ACKNOWLEDGMENTS

So many people made this book a reality by offering kind words, encouragement, and lending an ear when I needed it most.

Thank you first and foremost to my husband, Nick, for helping me plant everything from flowers to new ideas to wild adventures.

Thank you to Alyssa Jennette, my literary agent, for encouraging me and going to bat for me, and for your honesty and kindness.

Thank you to the whole team at Andrews McMeel, especially my editor, Melissa Rhodes Zahorsky.

Thank you to Stacy Fahey, Sarah Parker, and Kayla Stark, for working long hours with me with little complaint or question. Your friendship and encouragement means the world to me.

Thank you to Molly, who makes sure I never work for too long without a walk outside.

Lastly but never least, thank you to Muriel and Richard, my loving parents, who always believed in me. You inspired my fascination with plants through mandatory Sunday afternoon gardening.

INDEX

By Meaning

Passionflower . . . *Faith*

Protea . . . *Transformation*

Queen Anne's Lace . . . *Sanctuary*

Rosemary . . . *Remembrance; Wisdom*

Snowdrop . . . *Consolation; Hope*

Yarrow . . . *Cure for a broken heart*

FAITH AND SPIRITUALITY

Baby's Breath . . . *Purity; Innocence*

Bluebell . . . *Humility; Faithfulness*

Carnation . . . *Mother's eternal love; Heartache*

Chamomile . . . Energy in adversity

Cowslip . . . *Winning grace*

Dandelion . . . *Divination; Fortune-telling*

Fern . . . *Magic; Secrecy*

Iris . . . *Valor; Wisdom; Faith*

Passionflower . . . *Faith*

FRIENDSHIP

Apple Blossom . . . *Preference*

Aster . . . *Daintiness*

Bluebell . . . *Humility; Faithfulness*

Buttercup . . . *You are radiant with charm*

Camellia . . . *Longing for you*

Cattail . . . *Peace and prosperity*

Clematis . . . *Ingenuity; Cleverness*

Cowslip . . . *Winning grace*

Crocus . . . *Cheerfulness; Youthful glee*

Edelweiss . . . *Courage; Daring*

Eucalyptus . . . *Protection*

Forget-me-not . . . *Forget me not*

Hawthorn . . . *Hope*

Heather . . . *Luck; Protection*

Hellebore . . . *We shall overcome scandal and slander*

Honeysuckle . . . *Devotion; Affection*

Hyssop . . . *Cleanliness*

Iris . . . *Valor; Wisdom; Faith*

Ivy . . . *Fidelity; Attachment*

Jasmine . . . *Amiability; Cheerfulness*

Larkspur . . . *Levity*

Laurel . . . *Glory; Victory; Success*

Lily . . . *Purity*

Lily of the Valley . . . *Return to happiness*

Magnolia . . . *Dignity*

Mint . . . *Consolation*

Mistletoe . . . *Surmounting all difficulties*

Monkshood . . . *Chivalry*

Oak . . . *Bravery*

Olive . . . *Peace*

Orchid . . . *Elegance; Beauty*

Pansy . . . *You occupy my thoughts*

Rosemary . . . *Remembrance; Wisdom*

Sweet Pea . . . *Thank you for a lovely time*

Sweet William . . . *Gallantry*

Violet . . . *Modesty*

Zinnia . . . *Everlasting friendship*

GRATITUDE

Begonia . . . *To repay a favor; A warning*

Honeysuckle . . . *Devotion; Affection*

Iris . . . *Valor; Wisdom; Faith*

Lily . . . *Purity*

Oak . . . *Bravery*

Sweet Pea . . . *Thank you for a lovely time*

Violet . . . *Modesty*

Wheat . . . *Riches; Abundance*

Zinnia . . . *Everlasting friendship*

GRIEF AND SYMPATHY

Asphodel . . . *My regrets follow you to the grave*

Azalea . . . *Fragility; Temperance*

Carnation . . . *Mother's eternal love; Heartache*

Chamomile . . . *Energy in adversity*

Chrysanthemum . . . *Condolences*

Cypress . . . *Death; Mourning*

Forget-me-not . . . *Forget me not*

Gladiolus . . . *You pierce my heart*

Hawthorn . . . *Hope*

Hemlock . . . *Death*

Lily of the Valley . . . *Return to happiness*

Marigold . . . *Grief*

Mint . . . *Consolation*

Pansy . . . *You occupy my thoughts*

Poppy . . . *Eternal sleep*

Snowdrop . . . *Consolation; Hope*

Willow . . . *Mourning*

Yarrow . . . *Cure for a broken heart*

HEARTBREAK

Anemone . . . *Forsaken love*

Azalea . . . *Fragility; Temperance*

Basil . . . *Hate*

Camellia . . . Longing for you

Carnation . . . *Mother's eternal love; Heartache*

Chamomile . . . *Energy in adversity*

Chrysanthemum . . . *Condolences*

Cypress . . . *Death; Mourning*

Daffodil . . . *Unrequited love*

Datura . . . *Deceitful charms*

Gladiolus . . . *You pierce my heart*

Hyacinth . . . *Please forgive me*

Hydrangea . . . *Boastfulness; Heartlessness*

Lady Slipper . . . *Capriciousness*

Lily of the Valley . . . *Return to happiness*

Marigold . . . *Grief*

Rue . . . *Regret*

Snowdrop . . . *Consolation; Hope*

Tansy . . . *Hostility*

Thistle . . . *Misanthropy*

Willow . . . *Mourning*

Wormwood . . . *Bitterness*

Yarrow . . . *Cure for a broken heart*

LOVE AND ROMANCE

Apple Blossom . . . *Preference*

Buttercup . . . *You are radiant with charm*

Camellia . . . *Longing for you*

Chamomile . . . *Energy in adversity*

Cornflower . . . *Hope in love*

Dahlia . . . *Eternal love; Commitment*

211

Dogwood . . . *Our love will overcome adversity*

Edelweiss . . . *Courage; Daring*

Eucalyptus . . . *Protection*

Forget-me-not . . . *Forget me not*

Hawthorn . . . *Hope*

Heather . . . *Luck; Protection*

Hellebore . . . *We shall overcome scandal and slander*

Honeysuckle . . . *Devotion; Affection*

Ivy . . . *Fidelity; Attachment*

Lilac . . . *First love; Reminiscence*

Lily . . . *Purity*

Monkshood . . . *Chivalry*

Myrtle . . . *Love*

Orange Blossom . . . *Eternal love*

Orchid . . . *Elegance; Beauty*

Pansy . . . *You occupy my thoughts*

Peony . . . *Bashfulness*

Rose . . . *Love*

Sweet William . . . *Gallantry*

Tulip . . . *I declare my love for you*

PARENTS AND CHILDREN

Amaryllis . . . *Pride*

Aster . . . *Daintiness*

Baby's Breath . . . *Purity; Innocence*

Bluebell . . . *Humility; Faithfulness*

Carnation . . . *Mother's eternal love; Heartache*

Crocus . . . *Cheerfulness; Youthful glee*

Daisy . . . *Innocence; Childhood; Purity*

Eucalyptus . . . *Protection*

Heather . . . *Luck; Protection*

Lily . . . *Purity*

Myrtle . . . *Love*

Queen Anne's Lace . . . *Sanctuary*

WARNING AND DISPLEASURE

Basil . . . *Hate*

Begonia . . . *To repay a favor; A warning*

Belladonna . . . *Silence*

Buttercup . . . *You are radiant with charm*

Columbine . . . *Foolishness*

Datura . . . *Deceitful charms*

Fern . . . *Magic; Secrecy*

Foxglove . . . *Riddles; Secrets*

Hellebore . . . *We shall overcome scandal and slander*

Hemlock . . . *Death*

Hydrangea . . . *Boastfulness; Heartlessness*

Lavender . . . *Distrust*

Magnolia . . . *Dignity*

Nettle . . . *Cruelty*

Oleander . . . *Caution*

Petunia . . . *Anger; Resentment*

Poppy . . . *Eternal sleep*

Rue . . . *Regret*

Snapdragon . . . *Presumption*

Sunflower . . . *False riches*

Tansy . . . *Hostility*

Thistle . . . *Misanthropy*

Wormwood . . . *Bitterness*

WELL-WISHES AND CONGRATULATIONS

Amaryllis . . . *Pride*

Apple Blossom . . . *Preference*

Carnation . . . *Mother's eternal love; Heartache*

Cattail . . . *Peace and prosperity*

Clematis . . . *Ingenuity; Cleverness*

Clover . . . *Good luck*

Cowslip . . . *Winning grace*

Crocus . . . *Cheerfulness; Youthful glee*

Dahlia . . . *Eternal love; Commitment*

Daisy . . . *Innocence; Childhood; Purity*

Edelweiss . . . *Courage; Daring*

Eucalyptus . . . *Protection*

Forget-me-not . . . *Forget me not*

Hawthorn . . . *Hope*

Heather . . . *Luck; Protection*

Hellebore . . . *We shall overcome scandal and slander*

Lady Slipper . . . *Capriciousness*

Laurel . . . *Glory; Victory; Success*

Lily . . . *Purity*

Olive . . . *Peace*

Passionflower . . . *Faith*

Protea . . . *Transformation*

Queen Anne's Lace . . . *Sanctuary*

Rose . . . *Love*

Rosemary . . . *Remembrance; Wisdom*

Tulip . . . *I declare my love for you*